Original title:
Witty Wormholes

Copyright © 2025 Creative Arts Management OÜ
All rights reserved.

Author: Zachary Prescott
ISBN HARDBACK: 978-1-80567-809-0
ISBN PAPERBACK: 978-1-80567-930-1

Laughter's Launchpad Through the Universe

In a cosmos where giggles can soar,
Quasars chuckle, as comets explore,
Jokes are the fuel, they ignite the night,
Stars wink at puns, oh what a sight!

Black holes grinning with a cosmic grin,
As laughter echoes where time can't begin,
Planets spin wildly, all in a twist,
Forget serious matters, we can't resist!

Asteroids dance in a silly parade,
Their space suits adorned with a bright charade,
Galaxies whirl in a merry embrace,
In this playful realm, we find our place.

Nebulas shimmer with colors so bright,
Creating a canvas of pure delight,
In a joke-laden expanse, we take our flight,
Warping through laughter, into the night!

Celestial Comedy Club

Stars twinkle in a cosmic booth,
Jokes fly like meteors, uncouth.
Planets sip on solar wine,
Punchlines orbit, feeling fine.

Saturn laughs with rings of glee,
Venus snorts, 'Oh, can't you see?'
Galaxies dance in a twisty rave,
Black holes hide, bright jokes to save.

The Paradox of Playful Planets

Mars threw a party, very red,
Earth kept losing its head.
Jupiter bounced on clouds of gas,
'Why are we here?' asked the mass.

Mercury joked, 'You're quite dense!'
While Neptune sighed, 'What's the suspense?'
Time skips on a cosmic slide,
In this universe, none can hide.

Asteroid Antics

Asteroids spin like tops, they gleam,
Creating a raucous space-themed dream.
Zipping by, they made a fuss,
'Hey, who's the king in this dust?'

One rock replied with a cheeky grin,
'Stop your whining, it's a win-win!'
Around the sun, they whirled with cheer,
'Catch us if you can, oh dear!'

Chuckling in the Celestial Sea

In a sea of stars, laughter blooms,
Galactic tides wash away glooms.
A comet splashed with playful grace,
Leaves behind a giggling trace.

Nebulas swirl, their colors bright,
Clapping hands in cosmic delight.
Constellations share a wink,
In this vastness, we all think.

Cosmic Carousels of Humor

Round and round the stars do dance,
With giggles caught in cosmic prance.
Jokes are spun on moonlit beams,
As laughter floats through celestial dreams.

Planets wink with wise-crack flair,
Shooting stars trade jokes in air.
Galaxies twist with comic grace,
In this vast and silly space.

Whirling Wonders of Wryness

Spinning through the void so wide,
Sassy quips and jokes collide.
Asteroids toss puns like pearls,
In the midst of cosmic swirls.

Nebulas chuckle, colors bright,
Gags abound in the starry night.
With each spin, a new delight,
Laughing echoes take their flight.

The Comet's Chuckling Path

Comets dash with sparkling tails,
Leaving trails of jolly gales.
In their wake, the giggles bloom,
Brightening the quiet gloom.

Each atom sings a funny song,
As they whirl and whirl along.
Gravity bends with a hearty laugh,
Cosmic jesters on their path.

Gags in the Gravitational Field

In the pull of gravity's charm,
Laughter gathers, keeps us warm.
Stars collide in playful jest,
Twinkling laughs from east to west.

Black holes hide the best of jokes,
While comets tease with cheeky pokes.
In this dance of light and fun,
The universe plays, never done.

Dimension of Delight

In a realm where quirks reside,
 Time trips over, trying to hide.
 Tickles of laughter fill the air,
 Joy travels fast, without a care.

Upside-down clocks spin with glee,
 The trees dance with pure esprit.
 Shoes left behind start to prance,
  In this silly cosmic dance.

Spaceships made of marshmallow,
 Ride the waves of a giggling flow.
 Comets burst with candy dreams,
 Raining laughter, bursting seams.

Here we find the quirkiest flight,
 Where silliness takes its height.
Who knew that joy could warp and bend?
 In this realm, the fun won't end.

Serendipitous Space-Time Shenanigans

Bouncing through the fabric of space,
We giggle at time's silly face.
Laughter echoes in every warp,
As stars twist in a joyful torp.

Jumping jests from star to star,
We frolic and flip, comedy bizarre.
Asteroids crack jokes on their ways,
While planets just spin in a daze.

A time machine made of bubblegum,
Zooms past absurdities with a hum.
Unicorns ride on beams of light,
Sprinkling chuckles, pure delight.

In this frolicsome cosmic spree,
None takes life too seriously.
For in the universe's grand design,
Laughter's the bridge, a rope divine.

The Laughter Loop

In circles we spin, a giggle chase,
Time ticks in an upside-down space.
Each moment a slide, a slip, a grin,
As chuckles, like whirlwinds, begin.

Bouncing off stars, we take a ride,
Swirling in joy, with hearts open wide.
The echoes of laughter never end,
In this loop, all sorrows suspend.

Jokes ricochet from moonlit skies,
While nebulae watch with twinkling eyes.
A funny face, the cosmos smiles,
With a comedy act that stretches miles.

So let's dance through this twisty groove,
In every chuckle, let spirits move.
For in the boundless stretch of night,
Laughter will always be our light.

Comedic Constellations Collide

When stars collide, it's quite the show,
A burst of laughter, a cosmic glow.
Galaxies giggle and wink with flair,
As humor spreads everywhere.

Cosmic comedians in astral heights,
Tell jokes that sparkle like meteoric lights.
Each punchline shakes the milky way,
Sending chuckles to dance and sway.

A supernova bursts with cheer,
Blowing out jokes for all to hear.
Space dust chuckles in sparkly swirls,
As laughter lights up the world.

In this stellar blend of mirth,
We find our joy, our cosmic worth.
So let's collide with glee and shine,
For in the universe, all should be fine.

The Humor Hidden in Helixes

In spirals where the laughter hides,
A twisty joke that time abides.
Eternal punchlines, never old,
Where every turn a tale is told.

Microcosms, winks, and grins,
Entangled minds where fun begins.
With every loop, a chuckle found,
In tangled threads, we spin around.

Each DNA a giggle snared,
In playful strands, we're unprepared.
When science laughs, the answer's clear,
A silly thought that beckons near.

So dance within these merry coils,
Unravel joy, where chaos toils.
In every twist, a smile gleams,
Our merry hearts embrace the dreams.

Giggles in the Galaxy

Among the stars where jesters play,
Nebulas burst in a comical display.
A comet's tail, a silly dance,
With laughter echoing from every chance.

Dark matter hides in cosmic fun,
While black holes gulp, and time is spun.
Galaxy giggles, quite absurd,
Echo in silence, must be heard.

Planets spin with jesting flair,
Spouting tales of love and care.
A universe brimming with punchy cheer,
As stardust tickles, drawing near.

Orbiting jokes, forever bright,
In this vast space, we take flight.
So let's rejoice as we explore,
In sparkling realms, there's always more.

The Playful Paradox of Time

Tick-tock, the clock's a clown,
Time loops and winks, it won't back down.
Yesterday's laugh and tomorrow's tease,
In this paradox, we find our ease.

Chronicles filled with snickers and jests,
Moments served as hilarious quests.
Tickling seconds, playful and sly,
In this time frame, laughter won't die.

Past, present, future, all in a game,
Where funny faces aren't quite the same.
A giggle here, a chuckle there,
In timeless circles, we spin with flair.

So leap through time, don't hesitate,
For each moment's a chance to create.
In every tick, a joke aligns,
The playful paradox endlessly shines.

Jestful Journeys Through Space

Come join the ride, it's quite absurd,
Through cosmic paths where joy is stirred.
Asteroids smile, with comets that play,
In this wacky circus, we swing and sway.

With telescopes aimed at humorous sights,
Galactic clowns dart through the nights.
A journey painted in colorful hues,
Every planet tells its own funny news.

Through starry fields of laughter bright,
Space travelers dance in sheer delight.
Quantum leaps of comic grace,
In every corner, there's joy to trace.

So strap in tight and brace for cheer,
Our journey through space is never mere.
With every lightyear, giggles expand,
In the theater of the skies, we stand.

Quirky Quasars and Cosmic Comedy

In the dance of stars, they giggle and sway,
Bright lights entangle in a cosmic ballet.
Quasars burst forth with a laugh so loud,
Like a cosmic joke, amusing the crowd.

Planets spin tales in a playful tone,
Nebulae chuckle as they roam alone.
A black hole's grin is a sight to behold,
It swallows up light like the best stories told.

Supernovae crack jokes that explode with flair,
Their brilliant display leaves us all in despair.
Gravity pulls on our sides, oh what a rush,
In this cosmic circus, we giggle and hush.

Galaxies whirl with a humorous twist,
Creating a universe where laughter can't miss.
Each star a comedian, with punchlines to share,
In the cosmic expanse, all is fun and fair.

Time Travelers' Trickster Tales

Oh, the time travelers, up to their tricks,
With gadgets and gags that can surely fix.
Dashing through ages, with clocks out of sync,
Each twist in the timeline, a cosmic wink.

In the Medieval times, they trade for a snack,
But give them a gadget; they're sure to look back.
Victorian bowties meet sneakers and flair,
Their laughter erupts through the frosty air.

With a snap of their fingers, the ages collide,
A dino in jeans gives a comical ride.
From future to past, they frolic so free,
History's chapters rewritten with glee.

As they zip and they zoom through time's vibrant lanes,
They chuckle at history's silly remains.
Every laugh echoes through eras divine,
Where past is a punchline and time is the line.

The Sassy Singularity

In the center of chaos, a sassy scene,
A singularity, bold, and quite serene.
With a wink and a nod, it dances around,
While galaxies giggle, making silly sounds.

A vortex of laughter in the fabric of space,
It pulls in the humor, a light-hearted chase.
Every quip that it gathers becomes part of the whole,
A swirling creation that tickles the soul.

From stardust to laughter, it connects us all,
Like a cosmic jester, forever on call.
Spinning tales with a twist, it bends time with grace,
A fun paradox in the vastness of space.

The sassy singularity, with charm and with flair,
Reflects our own laughter in its cosmic stare.
In this endless expanse where the funny survives,
We share in the joy that the universe thrives.

Jocular Journeys Among the Stars

Set your sights high, on a comedic ride,
Through space's vast realms, with giggles as guide.
Rocketing past where the humor ignites,
In journeys of joy, touching endless heights.

As we frolic through constellations so bright,
The starlit ballet ignites pure delight.
Asteroids throwing their own laugh-out-loud,
Making jokes about planets, drawing in a crowd.

With comets that swirl like confetti in flight,
And meteors shrieking with laughter so white.
Each twinkling star has a story to tell,
Of chuckles and banter, they do it so well.

So join in the fun, let your laughter resound,
In jocular journeys where humor is found.
Across the great void, on this wild, fun spree,
The universe laughs, oh so joyfully free!

Quips Through the Quantum

In the realm where logic bends,
A jokester plays, the fun extends.
With puns that dance through cosmic waves,
A giggle echoes in hidden caves.

Particles prance in a lively spree,
Tickled by jokes of relativity.
Each quark a messenger of delight,
Cracking wise in the starlit night.

Time slips by, a merry chase,
As laughter lights up the empty space.
Gravity's pull can't hold it down,
In this circus of the cosmic clown.

With a twist and a wink, the universe spins,
Teasing the space where humor begins.
So join the ride on this laughter's tide,
Where quips and curiosities collide.

Jests Across the Stars

Stars giggle in the velvet sky,
As comets zoom and planets sigh.
With a chuckle here and a chortle there,
Galaxies shimmer, humor to share.

In a nebula, a prankster waits,
Playing tricks on the planetary fates.
Saturn's rings twirl with fit of glee,
While jovial moons play hide and seek.

Black holes swallow but lose the punch,
As they try to devour a cosmic brunch.
A dark joke in the void, full of flair,
Leaving the universe gasping for air.

Laughter echoes in supernova bursts,
In a cosmic dance, humor immerses.
With each joke, a new star ignites,
Blasting comedy into the night.

Humor's Hidden Portal

Beneath the surface of space-time's skin,
Witty wonders begin to spin.
Portals open to realms of jest,
Where laughter's the treasure, a cosmic quest.

Through the threshold, a jester winks,
In the fabric of space, humor links.
Each quip a ripple in the great wide air,
As smiles pop up with a playful flair.

Light bends around the punchlines made,
In this laughter's realm, shadows fade.
A universe painted in chuckles bright,
Where every star shines with pure delight.

Galactic giggles and squishy space slime,
In this funny place, there's never a crime.
So journey through, let your spirit soar,
To find the laughter that's forever more.

Lighthearted Adventures in Infinity

In the vast expanse of endless dreams,
Where silliness flows in vibrant streams.
A journey begins on a comet's back,
Chasing giggles down an interstellar track.

Worms in tuxedos do a moonlit dance,
Twisting through galaxies, they take a chance.
Each light year traveled brings jokes anew,
With every wink, they conquer the view.

In infinity's arms, jesters play tag,
With stardust tickles, they never lag.
To explore the humor woven tight,
In the tapestry of the endless night.

So laugh with the stars as you wander through,
In this lighthearted sphere, you'll find your crew.
With each clever quip and friendly cheer,
Infinity's jest won't disappear.

Echoes of Laughter in the Event Horizon

In a place where jokes take flight,
Cosmic giggles dance at night.
Stars twinkle with a cheeky grin,
As gravity pulls us deep within.

Time bends and bends in ways so odd,
A pun slips by, we all applaud.
Darkness chuckles, makes us sigh,
While light beams giggle, floating by.

An asteroid cracks a funny line,
Planets laugh in syncopated rhyme.
Spinning comets in a wild drag,
Chasing laughter in a cosmic swag.

From the edge, we hear a gleeful shout,
"Life's a party! Join the rout!"
Through spacetime's twists, we swirl and play,
In this endless jest, we'll forever stay.

The Lighthearted Labyrinth

In a maze where nonsense reigns,
Jokes catch rides on silly trains.
Twists and turns make laughter swell,
Through corridors where humor dwells.

Each path leads to a pun-filled place,
With mischievous grins on every face.
Walls echo jests from days of yore,
As echoes bounce from door to door.

Questions hang like stars in flight,
"Why did the comet cross the light?"
The answer tickles, leaves you wide,
In this weird realm, there's nowhere to hide.

With every step, the chirps ring clear,
Laughter dances, drawing near.
Around each bend, a riddle waits,
Unearthing joy as fate relates.

Spirited Space Explorations

In a ship where silliness floats,
We sail through cosmic tales and quotes.
Alien antics make us cheer,
As stardust tickles, a cosmic sneer.

Navigating quirks with cosmic glee,
Our mission? To find the silliest spree!
Black holes guffaw at our jokes so bold,
While nebulae shimmer in stories told.

Planets swirl in a comical dance,
Galactic comedy, take a chance.
On Saturn's rings, we slide and spin,
Giggling hard as we jet on in.

Joy rockets forth at every turn,
Stars ignite with the warmth we burn.
For in this adventure, laughter's the key,
To unlock the wonders of the galaxy.

A Journey of Cosmic Whimsy

Blast off into the playful void,
Where laughter's the currency, joy's enjoyed.
Asteroids wear hats, comets sport ties,
In this zany world, everyone tries.

Whimsical creatures hop and leap,
Witty tales from stardust keep.
Through meteor showers that sparkle bright,
We chase the echoes of pure delight.

Galaxies twirl in a merry swirl,
While jokes rocket forth with a twinkle and twirl.
Each wormhole leads to a joke anew,
Where punchlines bloom like flowers in blue.

In this cosmic carousel, we take spins,
Rolling on laughter while the fun begins.
Through celestial skies, our giggles soar,
In this whimsical journey, we can't ignore.

Quantum Quips of the Cosmos

In a realm where time is bent,
A quark plays jokes with no lament.
Stars giggle, planets hum along,
While photons dance to a cosmic song.

Gravity pulls with a mischievous grin,
As spacetime folds, let the fun begin!
Einstein chuckled from his seat,
Saying, 'Laughter makes the atoms meet!'

Across the void, comets chase,
With tails that leave a silly trace.
Nebulas blush in shades of blue,
Sparking wit as they bloom anew.

At black holes, where all is lost,
A punchline swirls, no matter the cost.
In the void, humor takes its stand,
Tickling the cosmos with a gentle hand.

Spirals of Sarcastic Stardust

In the galaxy's swirling embrace,
Stars exchange a smirking face.
A supernova winks in delight,
As meteors prank in the dead of night.

Across the Milky Way's wide arc,
Asteroids chuckle, creating a spark.
Jupiter nods with a jovial cheer,
While Venus throws shade, oh so near.

Saturn's rings pulse with laughter's tune,
As comets applaud, as if on the moon.
Quasars blare their snarky refrains,
While black holes roll eyes at the mundane chains.

In this cosmic comedy, nothing is grim,
Galactic jesters, each with their whim.
Stardust fizzes like pop on the floor,
While galaxies giggle, and ask for more.

Laughter in the Lattice

In the fabric of space, a pun unfolds,
Where neutrinos gossip with tales untold.
In a lattice of quips, we find our fun,
As laughter ricochets from sun to sun.

A photon struts with a swaggering flair,
Saying light years are just time to spare.
Binary stars share a giggling jest,
As they whirl and twirl, never a rest.

Whirls of laughter in cosmic dance,
Planets engage in a playful prance.
With waves of mirth in quantized streams,
The universe chuckles in playful dreams.

Through the dimensions, the jesters glide,
With ribbons of joy as their cosmic ride.
In this lattice of giggles, all is prime,
Making gravity feel like a pun in rhyme.

Cosmic Jests and Temporal Twists

Time is a loop, a playful ring,
Where seconds dance and giggles spring.
Past and future nod with a wink,
Creating moments that cause us to think.

A nebula grins, takes a comic pause,
As comets chuckle in star-studded laughter.
Puns echo across the light years wide,
As spacetime ripples, dreams we bide.

Wormholes dream of zany spins,
Where travelers laugh at their own wins.
Stellar mischief brews in every nook,
As the cosmos writes its quirky book.

Each twist of fate holds a witty glee,
With every quasar, there's fun to see.
In the grand scheme, we cogitate,
The universe smiles, it's never too late.

The Raucous Realm of the Stars

In the sky, with twinkles bright,
Cosmic jokes take flight.
Planets giggle, comets tease,
As meteors dance with gentle breeze.

A nebula winks, a starburst sings,
Galaxies wear the silliest things.
In this realm where laughter roams,
Asteroids knock on space-time homes.

Through the void, a chuckle floods,
A black hole gives out playful thuds.
Gravity plays hide and seek,
While the universe takes a peek.

In stardust laughter, joy is spun,
The cosmos laughs, let's join the fun!
In every corner, humor's found,
As the galaxy spins round and round.

Joyful Cosmic Conundrums

A riddle wrapped in starlight's glow,
What's faster? A wink or a flow?
Asteroids giggle in their clay,
As light beams chase them on their way.

Space-time puzzles, oh what a tease,
Planets play tag with the greatest ease.
With stars aligned in playful glee,
The universe dances, wild and free.

Quasars blinking, what do they mean?
Cosmic jokes that go unseen.
Through gravity wells we tumble and swirl,
In this carnival, we laugh and whirl.

Time may stretch, but our joy stays tight,
In comical orbits, we'll take flight.
From dusk to dawn, let laughter reign,
In the cosmic circus, we'll never wane.

Hilarity in Hyperspace

Warping through time, what's that I see?
A dancing photon, wild and free!
With zany speeds and giggles loud,
In hyperspace, we're joyfully cowed.

Light-years zipping, oh what a thrill,
A supernova burst, it fits the bill!
With each blink, the laughs grow more,
In infinite jest, we ever explore.

Cosmic clowns in a comet parade,
Chasing laughter, never dismayed.
Through worm-like tunnels, into the light,
Where every twist brings delight.

In this fast lane, we twist and twine,
Space is our playground, so divine.
With every detour and jolly prank,
In hyperspace, we'll laugh to the bank.

The Silly Singularity Chronicles

Gather round for tales so grand,
Of a singular spot that's unplanned.
There a quirk takes center stage,
Where chaos reigns, uncaged.

A space-time twist, a cosmic fling,
Where laughter begets a bouncy spring.
With every whirl, a giggle pops,
As light and humor never stop.

From black holes to gravity's humor,
Every twist makes a quirky rumor.
What's true? What's jest? It's all a game,
In this odd realm, it's never the same.

Through worm-like folds, we flip and spin,
In this silly tale, let's dive in!
With every turn, a chuckle roars,
In the chronicles, laughter soars.

Dancing in Dimensional Delight

In a twist of space-time grace,
Chickens cross to win the race.
Dancing through the cosmic beat,
Who knew the stars had such quick feet?

Jumping through a playful rift,
Cows on clouds just make a gift.
They tiptoe on the satin beams,
And giggle at our wildest dreams.

Planets swirl like disco balls,
While cosmic laughter freely calls.
A galaxy of jesters plays,
In unexpected, silly ways.

Comets wearing polka dots,
Chasing dreams in quirky spots.
Here, the universe is a spree,
Full of chuckles, wild and free.

Laughing Through the Light Year

Zooming past with easy flair,
Light years dance without a care.
Stars exchange their best dad jokes,
While planets share their quirky pokes.

Asteroids in tutus twirl,
Through space where comets softly swirled.
They giggle as they scoot and slide,
In a cosmic game of goofy pride.

Nebulas are cotton candy bright,
Creating laughter soft and light.
A universe where fun is key,
Whirling forth in harmony.

Each beam of light holds a jest,
In the galaxy's comical quest.
So, let the laughter lift you high,
As stars wink down from the sky.

Starry Shenanigans

Meteors racing, what a sight!
With a wink, take off in flight.
Galactic giggles spin and twirl,
As stardust shimmers, gives a whirl.

Planets pulling pranks on moons,
Singing silly, cosmic tunes.
Every twinkle hides a grin,
In this realm, it's fun to spin!

Saturn's rings are hula hoops,
While jokester stars play cosmic loops.
The universe hums a playful song,
In this symphony, we all belong.

Among the stars, the laughter thrives,
In these shenanigans, joy survives.
So join the dance, don't hesitate,
Embrace the fun before it's late.

Quantum Quips in Cosmic Currents

In quantum realms where riddles play,
Particles dance in a wacky way.
Entangled thoughts, a clever tease,
As atoms giggle with the breeze.

String theories hum a jolly tune,
Through the fabric of the afternoon.
Each quip a bow in space-time's thread,
Where ideas swirl and laughter's spread.

Curly creases and tangled loops,
Lead to giggles in cosmic scoops.
The universe shares a silent laugh,
As we ponder its playful craft.

So heed the cosmic winks and grins,
For in this dance, the joy begins.
Explore the quips that shimmer bright,
In currents of the starry night.

Jolly Joyrides through the Universe

In a ship made of jelly, we sail through the stars,
Past planets of pickles and chocolate bars.
With laughter we zip, like a comet on a spree,
Chasing space squirrels and giggling with glee.

Each twist in the cosmos brings tickles and fun,
We dance on the rings while we bask in the sun.
The Milky Way's sprinkles, like fairy dust bright,
Illuminate our path in the jolly starlight.

We wiggle like noodles in gravity's sway,
Where stars play hopscotch and planets delay.
With friends made of stardust, we romp and we roll,
On joyrides through galaxies, that's the goal!

As we twirl and we swirl in this carnival vast,
The stories of space are a hearty blast.
So come take a ride, leave your worries behind,
In the universe's playground, so silly and kind.

Elysium of Eccentricity

In a realm where the wacky is always the rule,
Dancing on comets, we play like a fool.
With a hat made of cheese and shoes of confetti,
We twirl in the skies, oh, isn't it petty?

Galaxies giggle, their laughter's a song,
As we prance with the planets, skipping along.
Unicorns ride the waves of the breeze,
In this quirky domain, we do just as we please.

The moons wear polka dots, the suns have a grin,
While the asteroids chuckle and spin with a spin.
Jumping through rainbows and somersaulting flies,
This realm of odd wonders is where joy complies.

With bubbles and sparkles, a festival here,
The universe winks, it's nothing but cheer.
In this playful dimension, we twirl and we play,
In the elysium bright, where oddities stay.

The Ha-Ha Horizon

At the edge of reality, where humor collides,
We find hidden treasures where laughter abides.
With comets that trip and black holes that chuckle,
We hitch cosmic rides, causing giggles and huddles.

The stars toss jokes like confetti on high,
And planets are laughing as time passes by.
Where quarks play hopscotch, and photons just tease,
The horizon's a canvas of whimsical ease.

With jokes on the table and puns on the vine,
We dine with the galaxies, sipping on twine.
As the sky bursts with colors, the humor unfurls,
In the cosmic café, we feast on the swirls.

So lift up your spirits and gaze at the sky,
At the Ha-Ha Horizon where funny things fly.
Join the merriment; don't be shy at all,
In a universe bursting with laughter's sweet call.

Mirthful Milestones in the Cosmos

In the cosmos's playground, we leap with delight,
With each milestone conquered, our spirits take flight.
The meteors dance as they twinkle and glow,
While space-time tickles where star rivers flow.

We drink in the stardust that sprinkles our dreams,
As laughter erupts with galactic extremes.
The universe whispers and giggles and spins,
Inviting us onward to see where it begins.

With every new journey, a punchline awaits,
As we share in the wonders, and open the gates.
To planets that wink, and suns that break bread,
In this carnival cosmos, let laughter be spread.

So gather your friends for this whimsical race,
In the mirthful milestones, we find our place.
With joy as our compass, and humor our guide,
We'll soar through the heavens on this cosmic ride.

Puns Among Planets

In a solar system, jokes do ignite,
When Mercury's fast and Saturn's in sight.
Venus makes quips, dressed in bright clothes,
While Mars tells the puns that everyone knows.

Jupiter laughs, a giant in size,
Spinning tall tales with twinkling eyes.
Uranus grins, though it's a bit blue,
Each planet's a punchline, each star has a cue.

Neptune just giggles, deep ocean of glee,
Spinning old yarns from around the cosmic sea.
With laughter that echoes through voids and dust,
In the grand universe, puns are a must.

As comets zoom by with a tickle and wink,
They stop for a moment, just to think.
In the dance of the orbs, a riotous flight,
Each celestial body brings joy, pure delight.

Gags in Galactic Gardens

In the garden of stars, where laughter does bloom,
A black hole winks, dispelling the gloom.
Quasars are chuckling, lighting the night,
While stardust laughs, creating sheer delight.

The meteors crash with a comedic flair,
Telling old stories as they tumble through air.
Gravity pulls in all those who dare,
But humor lifts hearts to float everywhere.

Cosmic daisies turn toward the sun,
While Martians argue on who's the best pun.
Asteroids clatter, they can't help but tease,
In this garden of whims, they do as they please.

With comical comets that race all around,
Each twinkle a giggle, each silence a sound.
In this vast galactic plot, full of cheer,
The gags flourish wildly, and laughter draws near.

The Zany Zone of Space

In the zany zone, where things twist and twirl,
Planets take jabs in a comical whirl.
Stars peek through clouds, with a twinkle or two,
And space dust dances, all merry and new.

Aliens jest as they float on by,
Their cosmic humor as vast as the sky.
With spaceships clashing in humorous bliss,
Who knew the void could hold such a twist?

Saturn pulls pranks with its rings all around,
While Pluto still jokes, though it's out of bounds.
Galactic giggles resonate so bright,
In this wacky realm, there's pure delight.

Journey through stars where the funny feels right,
A universe bursting with laughter and light.
In this zany expanse, where gravity's shy,
The joy of the cosmos will never run dry.

Mirthful Multiverse

In the multiverse realm, each world's a delight,
Dimensions collide in a riotous flight.
Time bends and flexes with a chuckle and grin,
As laughter erupts, new adventures begin.

Parallel planets exchange silly vows,
While doppelgangers giggle, embracing their brows.
In this sphere of humor, the more, the merrier,
Time-traveling jokes always seem to be scarier.

Lightyears of laughter drape across the expanse,
From jokes of the ages, we all take a chance.
Quirky timelines where no one is sad,
In this colorful dance, there's fun to be had.

Twirling through space in a whimsical spree,
The multiverse giggles, the fun sets us free.
So take a step forward, let joy take its course,
In this dazzling dimension, embrace the mirth's force.

Ticklish Time Travelers

In a clock that giggles, we took a ride,
Past centuries' secrets that they can't hide.
With each tickle of time, we burst into glee,
As history chuckles, come laugh here with me.

We met a knight who slipped on a pie,
A medieval mess, oh me, oh my!
His armor clanged loud, like a comical song,
As we rolled on the ground, it felt so wrong.

We danced with jesters in a carnival spin,
Their tricks gave us fits, oh where to begin?
With a flip, then a flop, they'd leap and they'd twirl,
In this merry-go-round of a time-travel swirl.

So let's steal a moment, a chuckle, a cheer,
And journey through time, with laughter so near.
Ticklish clocks and giggles will reign,
In the delightful dance, let's do it again!

Jesting in the Interstellar

In cosmic cafes, where stars love to prance,
We sipped on stardust, in a light-speed dance.
Beneath twinkling skies, we made silly bets,
With aliens laughing, as time forgets.

A Martian sang jokes about Earth's silly ways,
His punchlines like comets, a bright cosmic blaze.
With humor so vast, like a black hole's grin,
We shared in the joy that spun us within.

Zipping through galaxies, we tripped on a beam,
Finding slapstick moments in a space-time dream.
The moon winked at us, with a laugh that was bright,
As we floated on laughter through the endless night.

So come join the crew of the comedy stars,
Where laughter's the fuel for our ship that flies far.
In jesting adventures, we find our delight,
Across the vast cosmos, where humor ignites!

Laughs Beneath the Lightyear

Beneath the lightyear, our giggles collide,
With comets and quirks we can't quite abide.
A saturnine grin from rings that chime,
In this universe bursting with comedy rhyme.

A squirrel on a rocket, what a sight to behold,
Napkin notes tossed, all the jokes unrolled.
Through wormholes we tumbled, like marbles in spin,
With laughter galore, let the fun now begin!

As planets pranked each other with cosmic delight,
The stars burst with joy, in a twinkling night.
We surfed on the waves of a giggle-filled sky,
Soaring through space with a quirk in our eye.

From Milky Way jesters to nebula jest,
In the laughter of space, we've truly been blessed.
So strap on your humor and let's take a flight,
To laugh beneath starlight, oh what a night!

Planetary Puns of the Past

Once Pluto cracked jokes, he was small but spry,
In the circles of planets, he wouldn't be shy.
With humor astronomical, he took center stage,
As laughter erupted from every age.

Venus slipped jokes about Martians' stale shoes,
And Earth rolled in mirth at the bittersweet news.
While Saturn coiled laughter in rings of delight,
They chuckled through eons, deep into the night.

The asteroids joined, with their comedic hits,
In a cosmic gala, cracking up just a bit.
With slingshot progression through myriads of fun,
The universe laughed, making all chaos run.

So travel through time, and let laughter resound,
With planetary puns that spin round and round.
To the past, let's journey, where humor spans vast,
In the joy of the cosmos, forever to last!

Comedic Collapses of Continuum

In a wrinkle of time, a joke took flight,
A banana slipped past a starry night.
Quantum giggles swirl and sway,
As jokes bend the laws of night into day.

Gravity pulls but can't catch a grin,
As laughter erupts from where it begins.
Tickling photons, bouncing with glee,
In elastic time, it's a comedy spree.

The past trips on present's shoes,
While futures amble with silly news.
Puns drop like meteors, splatter with charm,
Warped space chuckles, causing no harm.

Dimensions collide in a fervent dance,
Twisting through space, giving humor a chance.
In this cosmic jest, nothing feels wrong,
As the universe laughs, a bright silly song.

Whimsical Whirls of the Universe

Galaxies twirl in a giddy parade,
Stars flicker and flap, join in the charade.
Spinning quarks with a sassy twist,
In cosmic ballet, none can resist.

A comet trips, stardust goes flying,
Planets hold hands, and they start crying.
With each little whir, they chuckle and don,
A jester's crown made of nebulous dawn.

Space-time tickles with spirals so bright,
Tick-tock, tickle, they're giggling in flight.
In every corner, a snicker is shared,
That even the black holes have always declared.

So glide through this cosmos, join in the cheer,
For laughter is cosmic, and it's always near.
In the orchestra of stars, let your joy swell,
As the universe spins, weaves tales to tell.

The Banter Between Black Holes

Two black holes met for a chat one fine day,
Exchanging some jabs in a light-hearted way.
"What's it like there in your singularity?"
"Oh, just dense thoughts and a great deal of vanity!"

"I heard you swallowed a star on a dare,
It vanished so quick, did you make it your heir?"
"Nonsense! It's gone, lost in time's cruel tease,
But I've plenty of humor, if you please!"

"I see your event horizon has lost its pizazz,
Should we hold a contest to get some pizzazz?"
"Let's throw a party for all of our friends,
And laugh as the light bends, just see how it ends!"

As they chortled and joked in their quirky little fold,
The chaos of laughter turned matter to gold.
For even in darkness where gravity's soul,
There lies a delight, a magnetic control.

Laugh Lines Across Dimensions

In the realm where the dimensions blur,
A pun popped up, like a silly burr.
From layer to layer, the laughter rang bold,
Knocking on doors of the time-space mold.

A twist in the fabric, a tickle, a tease,
Curving through paradox, bending with ease.
Each ripple of humor spills secrets untold,
And paints the dark canvas with stories of gold.

With popcorn from futures and snacks from the past,
They binge on the giggles, a cosmic repast.
The clock spins a yarn of eccentric delight,
As dimensions engage in a raucous night.

So dance through the layers, leap high with the jest,
For laughter in portals is truly the best.
Across the vast stretches, let joy be your guide,
With every new grin, let the cosmos confide.

The Joyful Journey of Jagged Edges

In a twisty route, we dance and glide,
Bumps and bends become our guide.
Jokes are tossed in the air so quick,
As we ride on this roller-coaster trick.

Through challenges that make us grin,
Every sharp turn leads to a win.
Laughter echoes where troubles cease,
In the jagged edges, we find our peace.

Bouncing back from every fall,
With a wink, we stand up tall.
Chasing laughter as it flies,
In our hearts, the joy belies.

So here we go, round and round,
With every twist, a new joy found.
Life's a game we dance along,
In jagged paths, we find our song.

Cosmic Jests in the Void

Stars twinkle with a cheeky wink,
As we sail on thoughts that sink.
Planets giggle at our plight,
In the vastness, there's silly light.

Black holes wear a playful grin,
Sucking in all our silly sin.
Galaxies spin a tale so absurd,
Where laughter spreads like a whispered word.

Asteroids shouting through the night,
Telling tales that spark delight.
In the silence of space, we sing,
Where cosmic humor takes to wing.

So grab your laughter, let it soar,
In the void, there's always more.
With a giggle, we drift along,
In starlit dreams, we find our song.

Echoes of Amusement Across Time

Time tickles with a funny tease,
Moments flit like dancing bees.
Past and future share a jest,
In echoes, laughter is expressed.

Ancient secrets with a chuckle spill,
As we ponder and get a thrill.
Present quirks and timeless quirks,
Life's a stage full of quirky perks.

History whispers in a playful rhyme,
Tricks of the past, a merry chime.
Gathered stories from every year,
Laughter lingers, drawing near.

So hold on tight, let's take a ride,
With amusing echoes as our guide.
In the dance of seconds, we find delight,
As time winks at us, infinitely bright.

Droll Dimensions

In realms where the silly sense prevails,
Dimensions twist like winding trails.
Every corner hides a jest,
In droll places, we find our rest.

Through portals of laughter, we leap and bound,
With prankster shadows always around.
Mysteries written in comedic lines,
In these dimensions, joy brightly shines.

Wobbly worlds where giggles grow,
And whoopee cushions steal the show.
Bizarre creatures with laughter to lend,
On whimsical paths, we joyfully bend.

So join this jolly, crazy ride,
In droll dimensions, come and slide.
With every twist, a laugh will bloom,
As we bop through this comical room.

The Nonsense of Nebulas

In a swirl of colors, so bright,
Stars are laughing, full of delight.
Planets dance in a silly way,
Who knew space could have such play?

The comets race in a goofy line,
Jupiter's moons share the punchline.
Galaxies twirl with a cheeky grin,
In the cosmos, the whimsy begins.

Asteroids chuckle, all bumpy and round,
While black holes tease, never to be found.
Supernovae burst with a ticklish flair,
In the universe, nothing can compare.

A dance on a neutron star's pointy edge,
Space is a joke, a cosmic pledge.
Where laughter echoes, oh what a sight,
In the nonsense of nebulas, pure delight!

Frolics in the Fabric of Existence

In the weave of time, we spin and sway,
Chasing shadows in a playful ray.
Lightyears leap, like rabbits in flight,
The fabric of life is a stitch of delight.

Wormholes giggle, peeking around,
Bending the rules, no logic is found.
Quasars winking with a twitchy tease,
Existence frolics with the greatest ease.

Each theory's a joke with a twist of fate,
Chaos holds court; let's celebrate!
Ticklish photons dance in the night,
In this fabric, everything feels just right.

So skip through the stars, don't be a bore,
Life's a giggle, with much to explore.
Embrace the crazy, the wild, the fun,
In frolics of existence, we all are one!

Galaxies of Giggles

In the spiral arms, the laughter rolls,
Each twinkling star has funny tales to tolls.
Planets play peek-a-boo in the dark,
Their jovial whispers send joy in a spark.

Shooting stars spread joy like confetti,
Cracking jokes while the universe gets petty.
Saturn rings clink like joyful chimes,
In galaxies of giggles, we share our rhymes.

A waltz through the void, oh what a spree!
Dancing through cosmos, just you and me.
Laughter floats in the starlit air,
In every corner, delight is laid bare.

Join the parade, the cosmic jest,
In this playground, we're truly blessed.
So spin with the stars, let your heart sing,
In galaxies of giggles, let the fun take wing!

Laughter in a Cosmic Bubble

Floating in space, a bubble so bright,
Filled with chuckles and pure delight.
Frothy stardust dances all around,
In this cosmic humor, joy is found.

The gas giants blurt out puns galore,
While moons roll on the cosmic floor.
Light travels fast, with a joke in tow,
Shining on worlds where the happiness flows.

Astro-nuts laugh as they bounce in glee,
While bright meteors crack smiles, you see.
In this bubble of fun, the void fades away,
Every moment is a sparkling play!

So pour out your giggles, let them expand,
In a universe that's perfectly planned.
With laughter around, in the soft glowing trouble,
Join in the joy of this cosmic bubble!

Chortles Across Cosmic Currents

A comet glides, a giggle spins,
Stars wink and toss, let the laughter begin.
In the vastness, pathways twist and turn,
Each chuckle's a spark, as pranks we discern.

A nebula dances, with snacks in tow,
Black holes munching on cosmic dough.
Planets wobble, they can't keep still,
As gravity jokes, gives a mighty thrill.

Asteroids chuckle, as they take a ride,
In the cosmic sea, they can't help but slide.
Skip past the sun, give Mercury a tease,
Galactic giggles carried on the breeze.

So leap through the void, spin faster, don't flee,
In this universal circus, we all are the key.
With each merry bounce, our spirits unfurl,
In the laughter of space, let joy twirl and whirl.

Anomalies of Amusement

Tickling the edges of time and space,
Jovial quirks all over the place.
Twinkling stars, they chuckle and rhyme,
In this riddle of distance, we're lost for some time.

A quasar shimmies, with a jazzy beat,
While supernovas boast of their cosmic feat.
Through wormy tunnels, we giggle and glide,
In this playful haze, there's nowhere to hide.

Galactic jesters juggling light,
Planets all spinning, a colorful sight.
As illusions form, and reality bends,
Come join the parade, where laughter transcends.

With each funny twist, a cosmic surprise,
Orbiting humor, through twinkling skies.
Let's ride the tides with a joy-filled heart,
In this anomaly, we'll never depart.

Tickle Your Orbit

Launch into giggles, our journey's begun,
Round and round, with every pun.
Alternating paths, twist and release,
A laugh in the void brings infinite peace.

Fluttering meteors join in the fun,
Gravity's grip? Just a playful pun.
Wobbling orbits, we'll dance through the gloom,
As laughter blooms like a star-filled room.

Comical comets with tails made of cheer,
Shooting through cosmos with joy, never fear.
Let's swirl through the spheres, twinkling in queue,
As mirth guides our way, like a bright, merry hue.

So bounce off the planets, let joy be your guide,
In this lighthearted voyage, take a giggly ride.
Together we'll float, through laughter we'll soar,
A jolly adventure, forever we'll explore.

The Silly Spectrum

In galaxies far, where humor lights beams,
A spectrum of silliness dances in dreams.
From red to violet, each color a laugh,
A kaleidoscope of joy, our cosmic path.

Fuzzy little UFOs playing hide and seek,
Zooming with joy, they're so very cheeky.
Asteroids giggling, as they fly by,
With every jest shared, we reach for the sky.

Light years stretch like a comical story,
As we whirl through the cosmos, basking in glory.
Each chuckle we share, a rhythm divine,
In this silly spectrum, we gleefully shine.

So gather your chuckles, let the verses ignite,
Cosmic humor awaits, in the deep starry night.
We'll navigate joy, skip puzzles with flair,
In this universe wide, laughter fills the air.

Comedic Collisions of Celestial Bodies

In the vastness of space, stars have a ball,
Joking with comets that zoom and then stall.
One nebula whispers, while planets all cheer,
"Gravity's weighty, but humor is clear!"

Asteroids tumble with giggles galore,
As black holes join in, forever implore.
When suns have a laugh, they twinkle and dance,
While space-time erupts in a comical trance.

A meteor rushes, then stops in mid-air,
"Who needs a ticket? I'm already there!"
In this cosmic circus, the laughter will swell,
As galaxies twirl in a whimsical spell.

So when you look up, don't miss all the fun,
For even the cosmos knows how to run.
With each twinkling dot and those brilliant rays,
The universe chuckles in most playful ways.

Splendid Silly Spheres

Round and round, they waddle with glee,
Spherical wonders, what a sight to see!
With laughter erupting from every great sphere,
They bounce through the cosmos, spreading good cheer.

Planets turn jokes as they orbit their suns,
"Who needs a map when you're having such fun?"
Galaxies giggling as meteors spin,
"Don't take life seriously, just dive right in!"

Each little moon with a wink and a grin,
Spins playful tales of where they have been.
In this cosmic comedy, joy's never far,
Just look at the sparkle of each little star.

So dance with the orbs, let your spirit fly,
In a playful parade across the big sky.
For laughter's the gravity that pulls us so tight,
In the realm of the spheres, everything feels right!

Riddles in the Radiance

Through shimmering beams, the riddles take flight,
Cosmic conundrums that tickle the night.
Stars play their tricks, with a glimmer and jest,
As they weave through the black, their humor's the best.

Planets exchange their most outrageous tales,
About comets that sing or black holes with scales.
A riddle unfolds from an old cosmic sage,
"Why did the photon refuse to engage?"

"Because it couldn't find a way to connect,
And light-years apart, what did it expect?"
The stardust erupts in a gaseous snort,
As laughter among them turns into a sport.

So when stars shine bright with a wink in their glow,
Remember their riddles, let laughter bestow.
In this endless expanse where no end is found,
The jokes of the universe resound all around.

Cosmic Amusements Await

In this vast playground where starlight bursts,
The universe beckons with giggles and thirsts.
Black holes do belly flops, with comets that spill,
While quasars are chuckling, bringing good will.

The planets all gather for games out of sight,
Playing hide and seek in the depths of the night.
"Come chase after me!" sings a star with delight,
But it's just a mirage; it'll vanish from sight!

Meteor showers rain down tales full of cheer,
With laughter that's cosmic, both far and near.
Galaxies link arms for a dance in the void,
Their joy spreading widely, that's never destroyed.

So look to the heavens, embrace the delight,
For cosmic amusements are shining so bright.
In this grand universe where all beings play,
Let echoes of laughter forever hold sway.

Parody in the Pulsar's Pulse

In the dance of bright stars, a jester will swirl,
With laughter in echoes, as comets unfurl.
The rhythm of light makes a giggle ignite,
While black holes are snickering, hiding their fright.

Asteroids chuckle, their orbits askew,
As cosmic clowns play a merry old tune.
They bounce off the moons, with a wink and a twist,
While planets roll over, reluctant to miss.

Gravitons giggle, a playful embrace,
As particles waltz in this grand, silly space.
The universe hums with a whimsical tune,
While quarks set the stage for a laugh 'neath the moon.

So let's toast to the chaos, the joy in the beam,
Where laughter and stardust unite in a dream.
A parody spun in the pulse of it all,
In the fabric of cosmos, let's heed the call!

Amusing Anomalies of the Astral

In the fabric of space, strange creatures poke fun,
With snickers that ring like a soft cosmic gun.
A nebula weaves tales with a delicate thread,
While time just trips over, bumping its head.

Quasars are jesters, with comets that glide,
Emitting a chuckle from deep in their ride.
With every pulsation, a tickle of light,
Creating bright rainbows from particles' flight.

Singularities curtsy with confusing allure,
Magnetics in laughter, the captivating lure.
Dimensions all wrapping in giggles galore,
As chaos and order both tumble and soar.

So slide in your seat, for the show's nearly due,
Where hilarity bounces on cosmic blue hue.
The anomalies merge, in a twinkling spree,
As space becomes wrapped up in joyous debris!

Banter Beyond the Blueprints

Galaxies whisper in playful exchange,
With banter that's cosmic, bewilderingly strange.
The models of matter all jiggle and shake,
As theories collapse in a laugh that they make.

Stars share their secrets in twinkling delight,
While graphs of existence take flight in the night.
Black holes roll their eyes at predictions so grand,
Sending out giggles across the vast land.

Measurements wobble, horizons expand,
Dropping their papers, no notes left to hand.
The universe snickers, it's seldom so still,
As equations break out in a fit of pure thrill.

So ponder the riddles of space without fear,
For humor's the answer, the punchline is near.
In the blueprints of laughter, we settle the play,
Let's script it together, come join in the fray!

The Ticklish Tesseract

In corners of time, where the silly does bend,
Lies a ticklish tesseract, fond of a friend.
With a giggle it flips, showing four dimensions,
While angles chuckle with wide-eyed intentions.

Cubes in a scramble, they dance all about,
While the corners are laughing, there's no shadow of doubt.
They wriggle in space, flutter shapes that delight,
Transforming straight lines into joyous flight.

Nonsense erupts as the fabric adjusts,
With playful banter, its quirks are a must.
On folding and flipping, it spins 'round the clock,
Inviting all minds to the humor it stocks.

So let's twirl through the loops, with a cheer and a clap,
In dimensions where laughter is the greatest map.
The ticklish tesseract beckons with glee,
A portal to fun, come and see what we see!

The Comedic Continuum

In a tangle of time, quite absurd,
A snail found a portal that blurred.
He zipped through the years,
With laughter and cheers,
Creating a ruckus unheard.

A cat with a hat danced in style,
Traveling realms by the mile.
It traded its yarn,
For a trip on a barn,
And cracked jokes with a grin and a smile.

Yet chickens were crossing the line,
Cackling backwards, oh what a sign!
They clucked about fate,
In a very odd state,
As they scrambled through space and time.

So here's to the quirks and the blips,
The cosmic parade and its quips,
For laughter's the key,
To unlock what we see,
As we waddle on interstellar trips.

Twinkling Tales from Time's Tapestry

Once a chair had a mind of its own,
It danced and it rolled, all alone.
In a loop it did spin,
With a giggle and grin,
As it claimed that the cosmos was known.

A toaster got zapped into space,
Making bread in a new time and place.
It popped out a loaf,
With a wink and a scoff,
Claiming breakfast was now an embrace.

A fish flew a ship, oh so grand,
In a galaxy far, far from land.
He told clay-dragon tales,
And spun up on gales,
While the stars seemed to wave a hand.

So here's to the laughter we weave,
In the fabric of tales we believe.
With each twist and turn,
May our hearts brightly burn,
As we chuckle and dance, never leave.

Jestful Journeys Through Spacetime

A frog on a lily pad leaped,
Into a time stream, oh how he peeped!
He winked at the stars,
As he juggled old jars,
And hopped in dimensions, well-heeled.

A mouse rode a comet so fast,
In a helmet, quite witty, steadfast.
He squeaked songs of delight,
Underneath the moonlight,
As he zoomed through the ages amassed.

The clock ticked and tocked with a grin,
As it giggled at where it had been.
With each wacky turn,
Laughter began to burn,
And reshaped the rules we live in.

Through giggles and glittering beams,
We spin on the edge of our dreams.
Let the jests fill the air,
With whimsy and flair,
As we float on the whirlpool of schemes.

Cosmic Chuckles and Spiraling Smiles

An alien chef made a stew,
From starbursts and comets, it's true.
With a giggle and dash,
He created a splash,
In a galaxy filled with the blue.

A robot told jokes, quipped with glee,
As it danced through the stars, wild and free.
With circuits in tune,
To the light of the moon,
It programmed the universe to agree.

A jellyfish in high heels glowed bright,
Floating through the cosmos at night.
With each sway and spin,
She danced on a whim,
Tickling all that came into sight.

So let's gather our laughs and our dreams,
In the orbit of joy, where it beams.
With cosmic delight,
We'll embrace the night,
And journey together, or so it seems.

Jovial Junctions in the Universe

In a twist of fate, a cat wore a hat,
Dancing on stars, how about that?
Planets giggle, circling in style,
As comets join in with a cheeky smile.

Asteroids tumble, a clumsy parade,
While spacetime wobbles, the whole thing's a charade.
Galaxies chuckle, quite light on their feet,
Stellar shenanigans are hard to beat!

Nodes of laughter between realms collide,
Gravity's tickle, nowhere to hide.
Join the fun, don't miss out on the ride,
In the cosmic playground, we've nothing to bide!

Orbiting jokes burst with cosmic delight,
Laughter expands in the vastness of night.
With stardust confetti, we'll soar and we'll twirl,
In jovial junctions, let's give it a whirl!

The Silly Singularity

At the center of chaos, a tumbleweed spins,
In the midst of a swirl where comedy begins.
Time wears a clown nose, it honks and it beeps,
While black holes giggle, in the cosmos they creep.

Dressed in a tutu, a neutron pirouettes,
Surrounded by quarks, engaging in bets.
Quasars are beatboxes, sounding out rhymes,
In the riddle of spacetime, laughter climbs.

The universe chuckles, so vast and so bright,
Where Schrödinger's cat takes a joyride at night.
In this zany expanse, forget all your woes,
As the cosmos composes a comical prose.

Through the fabric of space, with joy we'll traverse,
In the silly singularity, we banter and converse.
So buckle up tight, there's fun yet to find,
For in this grand spectacle, joy's intertwined!

Quirky Quasars

Up in the sky, where the anomalies play,
Quasars throw parties, who wouldn't want to stay?
Light-years of laughter, so bright and so bold,
In cosmic confessions, their stories are told.

Dancing in pairs, they waltz with delight,
Rockets flip-flop in the soft velvet night.
With the waves of a hand, they pulse and they beam,
Creating a ruckus, the ultimate dream.

A cosmic dance-off, it's quite the affair,
With galaxies munching on stellar despair.
Gravity's grip loosens, they soar and they glide,
In the realm of the quirky, there's nowhere to hide.

So join in the fun, let your stardust be free,
With quirky quasars, it's as full as can be.
As we spin through the cosmos, let laughter reside,
In the heart of the universe, let joy be our guide!

Traverse the Ticklish Tunnel

Down the ticklish tunnel, let's take a wild ride,
Where time and space giggle, forever allied.
Glimmers of joy sparkle like stars up above,
In the warmth of the void, we'll stumble and shove.

Through spacetime's breezes, a tickle ensues,
Among friendly neutrinos sharing their views.
As string theory dances, with twists and with turns,
We'll uncover the laughter that eternally burns.

The echoes of quips bounce off cosmic walls,
In the realm of the bizarre, where logic stalls.
With each giddy leap, we'll bounce off the walls,
In this ticklish tunnel, laughter calls!

So hold on tight, as we twist and we spin,
In the giggle-filled journey, it's time to begin.
Sailing through humor, with quantum delight,
In the ticklish tunnel, we'll soar into the night!

Laughter Beyond the Light Barrier

In a universe of giggles, we fly,
Curly mustaches, like comets, zoom by.
With each twist and turn, a chuckle erupts,
As silly space-time evenly disrupts.

With tinfoil hats and dreams made of cheese,
Alien dances that bring us to knees.
Bouncing around in the cosmic delight,
Forgotten time zones, our new favorite sight.

Gravity's whims lead us to laugh,
Even black holes take a comical path.
Stars wink in jest, a cosmic charade,
In this vacuum of joy, we're happily played.

Jokes in the asteroids, a meteor dance,
We're the punchline, given a chance.
As planets align, our giggles collide,
In the humor of space, we find our pride.

Jovial Nebula Navigators

Adrift in the clouds of a prismatic hue,
Navigating laughter, oh what fun to pursue!
We ride on the tails of bright meteor trails,
In a fuzzy cocoon where nonsense prevails.

Chasing stardust, a glitch in the mind,
With playful quirks of the universe, we find.
Galaxies spinning in a joyful ballet,
Each twist of fate leads us joyously astray.

We map out the giggles in this cosmic race,
Tickling planets with our silly embrace.
Dancing among stars, a whimsical theme,
In the nebula's glow, we live out our dream.

Sending out chuckles through the infinity beam,
Aboard our craft of laughter, we gleam.
From quasar to comet, we spread cheer and delight,
With every star's twinkle, our spirits take flight.

The Tickling Telescope

Through the eyepiece, a world full of glee,
Planets dressed up for a cosmic jubilee.
With a giggle on Mars and a chuckle on Venus,
Each twinkling light, a comedian's genius.

Fuzzy comets with mustaches and caps,
Galactic jesters play tricks and mishaps.
As we peer into space with a grin and a sigh,
Even the Milky Way wears a straw hat on high.

Viewing the cosmos through laughter's bright lens,
Nebulae whisper their secrets with friends.
Each starry clump echoes laughter we've shared,
In the vastness of space, no one is scared.

A telescope built for hilarious sights,
In this circus of cosmos, we share our delights.
From the edge of the galaxy, wild smiles we've sown,
In the universe's embrace, never alone.

Star-Struck Smiles

With a wink from the sun, our journey begins,
Through sparkling constellations, laughter spins.
Orbiting around with mirth as our fuel,
In the playground of stars, we're the jester's school.

Each supernova bursts with bright, joyful cheer,
Painting the cosmos with giggles sincere.
Dancing alongside the playful moonbeams,
In this stellar theatre, we're all part of the memes.

Asteroids chuckle, some float with glee,
Their rocky faces grin back at you and me.
In the warmth of the cosmos, our hearts feel so light,
Navigating joy through the vast, starry night.

As we frolic among the cosmic winds' swirl,
Even the vacuum hums a tickling twirl.
With star-struck smiles, we celebrate the flight,
In this galaxy of fun, everything feels just right.

Space-Time Shenanigans

A worm in space did take a trip,
Through cosmic bends, it danced and flipped.
It chuckled loud, defying fate,
In gravity's arms, it found a plate.

With stars to snack on, it feasted well,
Each twirl a tale, each twist a spell.
'Why walk a line?' it chewed with glee,
'I'll slip through time, just watch and see!'

As planets spun in dizzying rounds,
It cracked a joke, then fell to the ground.
'Time's just a noodle, swirling and twining,
A slurp of serendipity, so defining!'

Loop-de-loops in a cosmic game,
This wormhole gig had no sense of shame.
It slipped through jokes that tickled the night,
A wriggling laugh in the endless flight.

Satirical Spirals of the Sky

Snaking through stars, an amusing sight,
A worm with a quip, ready for flight.
'Time's just a joke,' it gleefully cried,
As comets zipped by, just laughing inside!

It tumbled through orbits with style and flair,
In a universe ripe for cosmic despair.
'Oh look at that planet, so round and bright!
Bet it spins tales of frolic each night!'

Galaxies giggled at its witty schemes,
For humor was woven in all of their dreams.
Each twist a pun, each turn a jest,
In this swirling dance, they all felt blessed.

With a playful flick, it changed its course,
A frog in space? No, a worm with force!
Dancing with meteors in cosmic delight,
Spinning out laughter, oh what a sight!

Punchlines Lost in the Cosmos

A comet named Zing sailed by with a cheer,
While a worm spun quips in the interstellar sphere.
'What do you call stars that can't pick a lane?
Rather star-crossed lovers, lost in their game!'

The black holes chuckled, a swirling spree,
As gravity played tricks in cosmic glee.
'Why did the asteroid cross the vast space?
To get to the punchline, a comical chase!'

Nebulas blinked like they knew the score,
As wormtail twirled, wanting to explore.
'I'm not just a worm, I'm a cosmic delight,
Dropping punchlines faster than light!'

In the void, laughter was a steady stream,
As stars erupted in a whimsical dream.
A wiggling worm with a heart full of jest,
Finding the funny is truly the best!

The Jovial Journeyers of the Void

In the depths of space, two worms went a-wandering,
Through swirling doors of time, ever pondering.
'Why work on the ground when you can soar?'
With giggles and grins, they began to explore.

A cosmic tavern where space-time met fun,
They played cosmic bingo beneath the sun.
'You can keep your orbits, I'll have a dance!'
With twists and turns, they led a bold prance.

On a comet's tail, they surfed and they slid,
Cracking up jokes, just space-kids they hid.
'Who needs a rocket when you've got a grin?
We'll zoom through the stars, it's where we begin!'

The universe echoed with laughter so loud,
As these rollicking worms danced 'neath a cloud.
Journeying joyfully through infinite space,
Finding the humor in this vast, funny place!

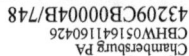

www.ingramcontent.com/pod-product-compliance
Lightning Source LLC
Chambersburg PA
CBHW051641160426
4320CB00004B/748